THE LONE WOLF
TYCOON

*A Guide for Introverts to Crack the
Code to Wealth*

Tim L. Gardner

TABLE OF CONTENTS

INTRODUCTION

Congratulations on downloading your personal copy of *The Lone Wolf Tycoon: A Guide for Introverts to Crack the Code to Wealth,* and thank you for doing so! If you are an introvert who is ready to start capitalizing on the common character traits of your personality, this is your book! In this book, we will examine some of the common character traits of introverts and explore how these characteristics became the building blocks to success that led some famous introverts to make their millions!

The first chapter will cover an overview of what it means to be an introvert, and cover how beneficial this personality type can be in today's marketplace. Some of the most successful entrepreneurs of our time are introverts; this chapter will introduce you to them and the introvert character traits that aided them in securing their wealth and fame.

The second chapter will begin the dissection of character traits listed in the first chapter. Humility, a common character trait of the introverted, will be the focus of this chapter. We will discuss how a quiet voice can roar, and how to be "boldly humble." You will be given an example of how being a calm yet secure person can have a bigger impact on the world than one could ever imagine.

Moving on from humility, the third chapter will discuss how self-sufficiency, another common character trait of the introverted, can become empower one enough to be able to provide for others. Becoming a self-sufficient individual is something that everyone strives for, this chapter will detail why it is so important.

Making the best of solitude is another common character trait of the introverted, and it will be the topic of the fourth chapter. To be introverted is to re-energize while alone. Introverts make the most of their time alone. If you are not already making the best of your alone time, this chapter will inspire you to begin doing so. This chapter will also break down how to budget your life, which is key to financial success.

The fifth chapter will cover the introvert's natural creative tendencies, and what they could mean monetarily. Most introverts have a creative outlet which they enjoy exploring; if this is the case for you, this chapter will give you examples of how best to fan that natural spark into a raging fire.

The sixth chapter will cover being goal oriented, another natural inclination of the introvert. If you are not the super creative type but your planners and calendars could rival that of any CEO, you already have a great natural tendency that can prove extremely lucrative with the right guidance.

Once you are making the best of your alone time, creatively or otherwise, we will discuss how to make the best of your time in public. Chapter seven will cover an introvert's natural inclination for observation. Introverts are very often described as extremely observant in public situations. Instead of focusing on making themselves the center of attention, as is the method of the extrovert, the introvert scans his or her surroundings, analyze everything and making calculations on how best to proceed. This is another of the most profitable traits of the introvert; the chapter will explore this.

Finally, once you have reached your status as a lone wolf tycoon, chapter eight will give you important advice about staying there and thriving as a successful introvert.

It is my genuine hope in writing this book that by the time you get finished reading, you realize your full potential and are inspired by those introverts around you that have tasted great successes. By the time you have reached the end of these pages, you should have a much firmer foundation from which to build your empire!

There are plenty of books on this subject on the market, thanks again for choosing this one! Every effort was made to ensure it is full of as much useful information as possible. Please enjoy!

CHAPTER 1

INTROVERSION AND SUCCESS

Once upon a time, business was all done face to face. A businessman was gauged on his ability to present himself to his customers and extroverts ruled the business world. Boisterousness was a key to success. One had to be loud to be heard and it was necessary to be in order to be effective. Gregariousness was almost a required trait to be successful in the business realm up until about the 1970s. It was then that things began to change. In this book, we will be all of these things (boisterous, gregarious and outgoing) while remaining true to the traits that give introverts the upper hand when it comes to success in today's business world.

As technology evolved, a whole new business realm was created. In the '80s and '90s, businesses developed by introverts were becoming mainstream. Men like Bill Gates and Michael Dell are only a few of the introverts that reached phenomenal success during these years. And, the success of introverts was not only limited to the tech boom of the 80's and beyond. The meek were taking the world by storm in a wide variety of industries. With the popularity of the public internet rising in the 1990's, Marc Seriff, Steve Case, and Jim Kimsey hit a big home run with America Online, and by the early 2000s, even more introverts were becoming more and more successful in the tech industry. Mark Zuckerberg began his meteoric rise to wealth with Facebook which opened the door for Noah Glass, Jack Dorsey and others who started Twitter and Kevin Systrom, the founder of Instagram. These people all became phenomenally successful without rising through the ranks of some big company as a successful salesman to one day become the Chief Executive Officer (the success path of the extrovert). They became successful with their intellect. Today, in the late twenty-teens and beyond, there has never been a better time to become a successful introvert. The exponential development of technology will only create more and more opportunities for the quiet and shy to shine.

By now you may be thinking, "Okay, so it's our time. Introvert pride! But how do *I* crack the code to wealth? How do *I* capitalize on my introverted tendencies?" Begin by taking an accurate assessment of your strengths. In this book we will discuss a list of common introvert character traits. If they are traits you share, this book will teach you how to make the most of them. If you do not yet possess all the traits in this book, then hopefully the explanation of them may help you unlock them from within.

If you are reading this book, the odds are likely that you believe you are an introvert. In this book, we will discuss some of the common characteristics of introverts and how they can be used to crack the code to wealth. Let's have a look the traits we will be discussing.

- *Humility*: One of the most common misconceptions about humility is that to be humble you have to yourself, or give others undue power over you. The truth is actually quite the opposite. To be humble one must be so sure of one's self that one does not seek out constant praise to feel secure in one's abilities. By the same token, if one is secure enough about the abilities one possesses, and is not so foolish as to believe one can do it all, one learns to take guidance and correction in stride with one's focus purely upon being the best one can be. Introverts' natural tendency to reflect often breeds humility, but if it is a subject with which you struggle this chapter will help you unlock its potential. Humility is strength. In this book, we will show you how to use it to your advantage.

- *Self-Sufficiency*: Another common characteristic of the introvert is the ability to take care of one's self. Because an introvert generally does not like to expose him-or herself to much outside persuasion, the introvert generally develops a strong sense of self-sufficiency. If this is not true of you, the chapter on self-sufficiency will surely inspire you to become more so. If it is one of your strengths already, or once it becomes one of your strengths, this chapter will offer guidance on how to turn self-sufficiency into the ability to gain a position of strength that will allow others to rely on you, in other words, success.

- *Making the best of solitude*: Introverts need to stop often and recharge their batteries. Spending time alone with your own thoughts or allowing your subconscious to process the thousands of bits of information you feed to your brain is an important time for the introvert. (Think of Superman and his fortress of solitude). It may seem like time alone cannot be monetized, as by definition money is a social construct, however, making the best of time spent alone is how an introvert gets ahead. We will discuss in this chapter how to tailor your time alone to become a lone wolf tycoon.

- *Creativity*: Since most introverts spend a lot of time alone, it is important not to waste the time and one common characteristic of the successful introvert is creativity. Whether it be music, painting, writing, gardening, or sculpting most of them find a creative way to spend their time of solitude. If you are introverted, and you dig deep enough, there is likely something within you that ignites passion. Some creative spark dwells within the soul of every introvert and it is all a matter of feeding it fuel to see it take flame. We will discuss ways to apply the lessons learned so far to make sure that your creative endeavors lead to a greater success whether by selling the art you create, playing your music for money or selling the fruits of your garden. If you are not the creative type, this chapter will offer insight into registering the ability to be creative within all of us, and a couple suggestions to help you bring that creativity to the surface. It is important not to waste time even if it is time spent alone.

- *Being goal oriented*: In order to succeed, one must plan to succeed. This is true of everyone. Because introverts spend so much time alone, there is often a lot of contemplation about what he or she wants to do with his or her life. A lot of introverts who are not as creative tend to be more studious and organized, so if your strengths are not in the creative fields, this chapter may feel more your speed. Regardless of where your organizational skills are, steps to outline and pursue your goals will be detailed, and by the end of this chapter, you will have a clear path to success.

- *Being observant*: Because the introvert is, generally speaking, "on the outside looking in" he or she generally gets a better idea of the bigger picture. While the extrovert is busy making themselves the center of attention, the introvert is scanning the room, gauging reactions and making calculations. The applications of this trait reach from being a better team player all the way to knowing exactly which strings to pull to make the puppet dance. The chapter on being observant will help you make the best of your introverted tendency to carefully observe the world around you.

Throughout the chapters, examples will be given of famous introverts so you know you are in good company. Wisdom from self-proclaimed introverts such as Warren Buffett, Bill Gates, Mark Zuckerburg and J.K. Rowling will be shared to help you set your sights on climbing the heights they have. Inspiration from Albert Einstein and Rosa Parks will show you how even the meek and mild mannered can make impacts on the world that last for generations.

The final chapter of this book will help you maintain success once you have tasted it. It can be overwhelming at times to go from struggling to being successful, and sometimes the path ahead becomes blurry. This chapter's checklist will help you make sure you stay on the path you have set out upon. By the end of this book, you will have all the tools you need to crack the code to wealth and become your very own lone wolf tycoon!

CHAPTER 2

BECOMING BOLDLY HUMBLE

T he term "boldly humble" may seem paradoxical, but the truth is that a quiet voice can roar. Humility is often misconstrued as weakness but nothing could be further from the truth. It is a common misconception that to be quiet and still is to be unsure or incapable, but again, this is not always so. Oftentimes one of an introvert's greatest strengths comes from his or her lack of the need to be noticed. Because the introvert gains strength from within, they are less often found tooting the horns of their successes. This is not to say that they do not achieve success, simply that they do so without calling for the spotlight. The introvert is more focused on his or her next success than he or she is on waiting for everyone to acknowledge what he or she has achieved. This is in and of itself an example of how humility can actually speed up the rate of achievements coming to fruition, yet there is more to it than just this.

Being overly confident in one's abilities can lead to disaster. When one claims greatness to impress a crowd and fails to deliver, how much more negativity ensues for their grandstanding? Working in the shadows to accomplish the thankless may seem less than desirable, but it is in the small, quiet, daily victories that life is lived. The humble man knows that he has worth without having to be told so by others simply because the humble man knows his work is worth doing. To be humble does not mean to not take pride in your work, pride and humility are not mutually exclusive. To be humble is all about recognizing your *actual* merits, giving yourself credit where credit is due, and not a bit more or less.

It is another common misconception about humility that to be humble is to beat yourself down in front of others. Again, nothing could be further from the truth. To be humble is not about downplaying your abilities; it is merely the lack of exaggeration and showboating. You do not have to claim worthlessness - in fact, the act of being successfully humble dispels any doubts as to your worth. To become more and more confident in one's skills and abilities and inherent worth is how one goes from being merely humble to being boldly humble.

An example of bold humility is found in the story of Rosa Parks, a civil rights activist from the mid-1900s. Rosa Parks was not the loudest protester, nor a passionate speech maker,

Rosa Parks was in fact widely described as being mild-mannered and meek. While others were fighting for social justice in their own ways, Rosa Parks' security of self set the stage for some of the greatest change to occur in American history. Rosa Parks, a black woman, would not give up the seat she was sitting in to white passengers who had just boarded the bus. She was approached with the ideologies of the time: "you have to move because these white people deserve your seat; they are worth more than you." She politely disagreed, refusing to move, asserting her worth by passively resisting. She did not cause a violent scene when she was taken into custody, it all happened without her making a fuss. Her actions were loud enough, she had no use of loud words. The effects her simple acts have had still echo throughout our society to this day. One woman refusing to sell herself short changed the world.

Rosa Parks was not rich, and she was by no means a tycoon, but she is possibly the best example of how a sure-minded, humble person can make a huge impact on the world. The reality of wealth is that to accrue massive amounts of it, one must change the world. Sometimes, however - as in Rosa Parks' case - that change does not come with monetary wealth attached. It is, nonetheless, notable that the fame of her name has lived for generations, and the worth she created in the minds of some of society's most downtrodden members is not without value. It is, of course, the goal of this book to give you the tools you will need to crack the code to wealth in a financial sense, and to that end, this lesson of humility is still an important one to learn. To be humble, to be securely firm in self-worth without the need to express it constantly, is one of the greatest tools you can take with you into any job. Actions speak louder than words; bragging is a fool's errand. Capability and worth will be determined by your employer, therefore performing your duties diligently and effectively is far more demonstrative of your value to the company than constant self-praise. It is better to be unexpectedly impressive than to fall short of promises made in haste.

Another great example of a humble person with great power and also financial success is Warren Buffet. He is widely considered to be the most successful investor in the world, worth about $66 billion, yet still lives the same humble lifestyle that he did before becoming a billionaire. He has lived in the same house in Omaha NE that he bought in 1958.

As an introvert, your inclination will be to stay out of the spotlight. This general sense of humility will keep you from making a fool out of yourself in most situations, but one of the downsides is the fact that it can leave you overlooked. This is where you must learn to be boldly humble. To be boldly humble, you have to build upon the strengths revealed through humility. For example, let's say you have a weekly sales invoice to complete, and because you keep your data organized and are quick at math you consistently turn it in before the end of the day that it is due, never turning it in late. If you procrastinate completing it because you know you can complete it in a short amount of time, your skills are not being showcased. If you were to make sure that the invoice is completed by the night before it is due and then turn it in first thing in the morning, your abilities would begin to shine. After a few weeks of being the first to turn the invoice in, you will begin to stand out among your coworkers. After a few months of consistently turning your work in first, your name will stand out when your employers begin considering who to promote within the company. This example is fairly specific, but the point is universal: act to achieve the best outcomes possible in your line of work and your employers will take note of their own. This is the secret to being boldly humble: you will not have to toot your own horn if others are singing your praises.

CHAPTER 3
SELF-SUFFICIENCY AND BEYOND

P art of being humble, part of being *able to be* humble, is the ability to take care of one's self. Being self-sufficient, being self-motivated, is another character trait of the introvert that is highly sought after in the professional world. Most bosses do not want to have to micromanage their companies or their employees. They expect that the people they hire to work for them are going to be able to accomplish the tasks they are assigned without having to constantly be checked on. Self-sufficiency in an individual is akin to reliability, and everyone who has people working for them wants to know their team is reliable.

Introverts are known to be mostly self-sufficient. There are rare cases of co-dependent introverts who rely heavily on others for emotional or financial support, but in most cases, the introvert takes care of his or her own needs. The degree to which one is self-sufficient can fluctuate, so one must constantly be reviewing one's needs in order to make sure that they are being met. Realistic self-assessment is key to making sure that one is being efficient in all one does.

Being self-sufficient does not always mean that you have to take care of every aspect of an accomplishment yourself, though. If you go to a restaurant and have a meal cooked for you, but you pay for it with money you have earned, you are still being self-sufficient even though you are not completing every task that needs to be completed. You do not cook the food, you do not wash the dishes, but you get fed because you have earned the money. This network of efficient members— the cook, the dishwashers, the servers—is an example of how when self-sufficient people work together, life goes as planned. This is what employers are looking for: self-sufficiency is akin to reliability, reliability is efficiently effective. Someone who is taking care of their responsibilities will inevitably bring success to their companies.

In truth, self-sufficiency is the first real step one takes to becoming a lone wolf tycoon. Everyone has to start somewhere, and this rung near the bottom is the first one that one must get a grip on to begin one's climb of the corporate ladder. See, if you expect to be able to manage a team, you are going to have to know how to cater to their strengths, weaknesses, and needs. For you to know the strengths and weaknesses of your individual team members, you will have to get to know them, but their needs need not be a puzzle. If you are self-sufficient, you can know what someone needs before they do, because you know what *you* would need in their situation. For example, let us say you are an oil service technician. You know that to change the oil in a car, you will need certain tools to get the old oil filter off, something to collect the old oil in, a new filter to put back on, and new oil to put into the car. Every car is going to require just a little bit of a tweak of the variables, but the general idea is the same. If you were the self-sufficient kind of person, you would know where each kind of filter is, where the new oil is, and you would make sure to have your tools and collection pan at the ready. A self-sufficient person is an efficient person, you would more than likely have everything you need in an accessible place before you begin your work. This would drastically reduce the time it would take you to complete jobs, meaning you would make your company more money per hour than someone who may never take the time to ensure their space is as streamlined as possible. Remembering to be humble, you would simply be rolling through jobs, continuing to pop up to your bosses with a "Hey, my bay is clear, roll me another one in!" Your bosses would begin to take notice, and you would likely be given instruction in educating your coworkers to be more efficient. You would be tasked with sharing your knowledge of self-sufficiency, and may even be given the responsibility of managing your coworkers to ensure they continue to operate at the standards you hold yourself to. This is, of course, another fairly specific example, but the truth contained is valid: being self-sufficient, paired with being humble, is a fantastic way to ensure that your presence in the workforce is noticed, respected, and eventually strongly desired.

Self-sufficiency does not mean having all the answers either, though. Sometimes it means just being willing to ask the questions. Warren Buffett, the famous philanthropist and financial leader, is an example of a man who recognized his limits, then set out to surpass them. He is a self-professed introvert, yet he is wildly successful in the business realm and became so during a time when business was the extrovert's game. How? Because when he realized he needed to expand his list of abilities, he took it upon himself to register for seminars to learn more about public speaking. He was a man who already had immense talent for sniffing out the best investment opportunities, but he knew that he had areas in which he could improve, so he did just that: improved. His success, fame, and wealth are examples of why you should strive to be as self-sufficient as possible. The term lone wolf tycoon insinuates the ability to take care of yourself, and if ever there was any question as to why, look no further than Warren Buffett's immense success for answers.

CHAPTER 4

SOLITUDE: THE INTROVERT'S BEST FRIEND

I f there is one single defining characteristic of the introvert it is that the introvert loves their time alone. While an extrovert gets their energy from being the center of attention, the introvert is no more at home than when he or she is completely alone. Whether it is in your favorite chair with a great new book, or on the couch watching your sixth episode of a new show, or in bed simply browsing social media on your phone or computer, if you are an introvert home truly is where the heart is. It may seem that simply recharging is the best use of your time alone, but if your goal is to become a lone wolf tycoon, cracking the code to wealth will require that you aggressively pursue your empire. This does not mean that you are not to relax and enjoy your time alone, far from it. More often than not, the periods of solitude spent in rest and relaxation are just what you need to get back out there in full force, just remember to never lose focus. We will go over being goal oriented in a future chapter, but in this chapter, we will discuss one of the most beneficial ways to spend your time alone: budgeting. Being humble and self-sufficient are activities that are generally more geared towards your time with others, though they have applications in the solitary times in your life as well. Since we have already discussed these concepts, let's go over how to apply them to your solitude before moving on to discussing how to budget.

There are many ways to define a humble home, ranging from complete deprivation to minimalism, but the most realistic and useful application of being humble at home is to simply live within your means. Can't afford that 60-inch tv? Don't go rent it and pay three times more than it is worth just so you can have it right then and there. Buy yourself something you can afford, and use the lack of everything you cannot afford as the motivation to drive you to get to a financial place where you *can* afford everything your heart desires. Live as comfortably as possible, and open lines of credit to build your credit, but do not dig yourself holes you cannot get out of just to have the latest gizmos. This is honestly essential if you are going to be a tycoon, lone wolf or not! Money management is pivotal to accruing wealth, so be smart with your money and humble with your home.

On the self-sufficient side of home life, making sure that all your needs are met at home is important to ensure that you will be able to function at your best in society. The introvert recharges his or her batteries at home, so home must be the recharging kind of place. Ensuring that you keep yourself stocked with amenities and plenty of food will ensure that you are able to take care of yourself most properly. A self-sufficient person will make sure all their bills are paid on time and their resources are stocked all times; this will lend the wall which you can press your back to when you need to feel secure. Being self-sufficient will require you to be accurately assessing your situation financially as well, and there is no better place to outline a budget than the comfort of your own home.

Money management is a great way to spend your time alone. Budgeting does not take a long time, but it is something you should be doing frequently throughout the day. When you are alone at home you can do your most hardcore budgeting, but you should be considering it while you are out and about. It is as simple as thinking to yourself "Can I really afford this?" To answer that question most accurately, you will need to develop a budget. Developing a budget is easier than it sounds, and since we have already established its necessity, let's break down exactly how to do it.

To develop a budget, you will need to know how much money you are earning, how much you absolutely *have* to spend, how much you need to save, and how much that leaves you to play around with. So, plan your month. Let's say you make $2000 a month. Rent is $500; utilities run another $200; food averages $100 a week, so $400 overall; car note and insurance are $320; you put $20 in gas in your car a week, so $80 overall; and your cell phone bill is another $80.

$2000	
-	$500
-	$200
-	$400
-	$320
-	$80
-	$80

$420

So after all your month's expenses, you have $420 left over to use how you see fit. You should always be putting a little money away for a rainy day, even if it is only $20 a month. If you make $2000 a month and you only save $20 a month, though, you are only saving 1% of your income, which is not a very high amount. At 5%, you are only looking at putting $100 away, and after a year you will have saved $1200 instead of $240. After five years of saving, you could either have $6000 or $1200. Think about it; denying yourself a little extra now could see you giving yourself something major down the line. If you put 10% of your $2000 away a month, after five years you would have $12,000 saved. That's half a year's wages!

After you decide how much you want to save, you can budget the rest of your money by deciding how much you will spend and on what, scheduling movie dates or maybe dinners out, or you can just keep that general number in your mind and be mindful of your spending to ensure you do not over-do it. If you have put away $200 of the $420, you would have $55 dollars a week to spend however you wanted to.

Budgeting is an important part of life, and one best done alone – however, it is not the only way that solitude can be used to get ahead in life. One of the most famous introverts, Albert Einstein, said of solitude: "The monotony and solitude of a quiet life stimulates the creative mind." Einstein has a number of quotes on solitude, and stories of his life never fail to detail the fact that he much enjoyed his solitude. He is even quoted as having said he had a "need for solitude," and it is no wonder why. His ideas, opinions, theories and formulas were groundbreaking, earth-shattering revelations about the world in which we live. His ability to see things in a completely new, yet undeniably true, fashion was a product of the fact that he spent a lot of time by himself deep in thought. His name is synonymous with intellect, so it may seem that his success is unattainable to the average introvert, but the lesson he wanted to share about solitude rings true regardless of how intelligent you may or may not be. His point about the need to be alone is that when you spend time alone you solidify yourself in the knowledge of your own world. This is not to say that you are to live in your own version of reality that is completely detached from the rest of society, it is more to mean that when you spend time thinking for yourself, by yourself, you are able to form your own opinions, ideas and theories about the world around you, maybe even coming up with your own formulas on how to operate within the world. For example, it is well known that social drama spreads quickly by word of mouth. Someone with less information about an event or situation may be inclined to share information as if it were the gospel truth, and that information may sway many minds to form new and more fantastic versions of itself before reaching your ears. If you intake some information that does not seem to register quite right and you sit quietly by yourself thinking about what you already knew and what you have just learned, formulating relativities between what may be and may not be true of both pieces of information, you can eventually form an opinion or theory on the situation that is based more on the truth within your own knowledge and the way you see it in than what has simply been presented to you. Your removal from society's clamoring can allow you the space you need to think, and the ability to form your own opinion or theory on the situation. By then taking your theory back to the population, even if it correlates with another's, you are able to add a personal addition to a public forum that has worth as being of your own creation.

This ability to recalibrate free of the public eye is enjoyed by every introvert. The most successful introverts use the time they spend alone to the fullest of its potential. There are many ways to make sure you are doing so, it will take your own personal reflection on your life to come up with the best way to use your solitude. Cracking the code to wealth is as simple as making the best of absolutely every single moment of your life. Being humble keeps you focused on the reality of what is needed to succeed, which is not constant praise. Self-sufficiency is the mark of a man (or woman) who is taking care of himself (or herself) and will eventually be taking care of others. Time alone can be spent a number of ways, but there are a few things one must do in order to succeed. Budgeting and thinking for yourself are two of the most important aspects of life that you must master if you are to become the most successful lone wolf tycoon. The best time to do either of those things is when you are alone.

CHAPTER 5
MONETIZING CREATIVITY

Most introverts enjoy their time alone because it allows them to express themselves free from the judging eyes of society. Some painters have no problems with letting others watch them work, some even enjoy teaching, but the majority of creative types enjoy exploring their passions in the comfort and solitude of their own homes. Self-expression is a very revealing act, and especially so when one is in the midst of creating a work of art, no matter the medium. It can also be an extremely lucrative experience, as good art fetches high prices. Famous musicians make millions of dollars for performing their music, but even local musicians achieve fame and financial gain by playing their local bars and venues. Master artists fetch millions for their paintings, but even local artists can make a living by painting commissioned pieces if their skills are good enough to be sought after. There are plenty of ways to capitalize on your creativity, let's go over a few.

Because we have expressed the need to be humble quite a bit, and by now you should be getting the point, its application to your creativity will be brief. Do not mistake intent, it is still extremely important to be humble about your work, It is just that by now you should be getting the picture of how important humility is in every aspect of your life. The humble artist's talent is allowed to shine without the taint of his ego. Anyone who is not creative enough to create what may come easily to the artist is naturally going to be a little jealous of their abilities. Left un-fanned, the flames of jealousy soon die down as admiration takes their place. Admiration becomes appreciation, and eventually what they feel for your talents is nothing but positive. If your attitude is pretentious, however, you can almost guarantee that it will have a negative effect on how people receive your artwork. No one likes a braggart, not in an office, not at an art gallery, not at a concert. If you feel like you have a bit of social ineptitude, it is best to just keep quiet and let your art speak for itself. If you play a show but have a tendency to put people off, accept praise with a smile and thanks, and socialize as little as possible. People will appreciate a little mystery a lot more than they would appreciate being talked down to. Again, being humble is all about being appropriate. It is a fine line to walk as an artist; one side craves attention but the other fears rejection. The best bet of making sure your art is the most well received is to let it speak for itself.

Self-sufficiency is an important aspect of introversion that actually has a lot to do with the monetizing of creativity. If you are going to make money off of your artwork, you are generally going to have to be the one putting yourself out there. If you are a musician you may have a bit of help from the rest of the band or a manager, but if you are a visual artist who has piles of paintings stacking up, you will have to take it upon yourself to get your work and your name out there. Luckily, monetizing creativity has never been easier for the introvert. Social media offers many completely free platforms that you can use to showcase your talents. Soundcloud is a free place to upload your music, and Instagram, Facebook, and Tumblr are all free ways to showcase your visual arts. With a little research—something more than familiar to all the self-sufficient—you can find the right way to break into your market.

The most important aspect of being able to capitalize on your creative talents is to never stop creating. J.K. Rowling is an example of how persistently pursuing your talents can lead to unbelievable success. Harry Potter has become one of the most common household names; the world he lives in was entirely fabricated by Rowling. She suffered many failures before penning the books that would skyrocket her to fame and fortune, but she never gave up on her passion. She has often talked about how introverted she is. She tells a story of how she was too shy to ask for a pen when she realized she had forgotten hers while riding a bus. Even though she later became one of England's most famous writers, she started out as a shy mousy bookworm who spent her days daydreaming. The lesson here is that daydreaming is a wonderful pastime when followed with a bit of creative output.

Now, maybe you do not consider yourself the creative type. You may enjoy reading books but could never imagine the possibility of penning the next great novel of our generation. In truth, it is not necessary to set your sights on the top of the mountain if you know you will never reach it. Creativity can be monetized to great success, but it has more value than simply being a way to make money. Creative problem solving is a term used for out of the box thinking in a workplace environment. It is a highly sought after character trait that does not require you to be good with a paint brush, and it is oftentimes found in introverts. The ability to come up with new and inventive ways of solving problems comes from the introvert's natural inclination to consider him- or herself in every situation. An introvert is more likely to consider how *he* (or she) might solve the problem, and less likely to look for others for guidance. This does not mean the introvert would not take advice, or ask if their solution has been tried before trying it, it just means that they are more likely to consider many options based on how they think they could solve the problem. It requires a knowledge of self to be a creative problem solver because one applies one's experience to a problem. Knowledge of self is very often present in the introvert, therefore they generally make very creative problem solvers.

So you see, creativity comes in many forms. Because of this, there are many ways to apply the concept of creativity in your life. The best way to expand upon your creative abilities is to create. If, again, you do not consider yourself the creative type, do not sell yourself short! Get yourself some puzzles to make in your alone time. While television and books are great ways to present yourself with new situations that you may not have encountered in your life (yet?), allowing you to form complex ideas and opinions based on information you may not have otherwise been exposed to, creative outlets give you time to reflect upon your own life in an engaging and enjoyable way. Puzzles are a great way to create art, as the finished product more often than not *is* a piece of art. You may not have created the artwork depicted, but spending time putting the puzzle together is a way to exercise those creative problem-solving skills. Finding the right way all the pieces fit is a great brain exercise, and when you have finished your contemplative creation, you can frame your accomplishment and decorate your home with it!

The monetization of creativity is as personal as the experience of being creative. If you are an artist, consider setting yourself up on social media. Research festivals and flea markets you can showcase your work in. Actively pursue the monetization of your talents, no one is going to do it for you! If you are a musician, make demos, visit your local bars and make your face familiar, get yourself on social media as well. The more effort you put into getting yourself out there, the more results you will see! And of course, if you are not the super creative type, explore the concept of creative problem-solving. Doing brain teasing games and challenging yourself with mental exercises like puzzles are great ways to get your creative juices flowing. You may find that the more you consider creative activity the more you find yourself gravitating towards some form of creative outlet. If you get the itch to pick up a guitar, give it a shot! You never know where your fortune may come from, so explore every avenue. Creativity fuels many industries, and the opportunity to break into any of them is only limited by the amount of effort you are willing to put into it. Chase your dreams and you may just catch them!

It should be noted that you should take care not smother your creative flames in the pursuit of living your dreams as a successful artist. Part of being successful at anything comes from the knowledge of when to go full steam ahead, and when to rest and recuperate. Creative endeavors are no different. Do not work yourself into the ground, you will never be successful if you do. Making the best of every moment requires you to accurately assess what needs to be done in each moment. For more on that, let's move on to the chapter on goals and reaching them.

CHAPTER 6

ON GOALS AND REACHING THEM

We have established many character traits that introverts have used to their individual advantages. Humility, self-sufficiency, an affinity for solitude, and creativity are all important pieces of the introvert puzzle. Making sure these pieces fit is achieved by the introvert's natural inclination to being goal oriented. When one knows where one is going, one is far more likely to get there. Success does not happen by accident, and it is generally by careful planning that it is achieved. The general division between the two kinds of people in the world goes "right brain/left brain." Right brain people are said to be more creative, left brain people are more organized and systematic. So if your strengths are not in the creative fields, take heart; there are still ways to capitalize on your talents!

Setting goals and making schedules are activities that most engage in, but there are those who feel they do not have the time or have no need of looking into the future. A lot of people get wrapped up in the present and life seems to slip by. If you are one of the people who considers schedules out of your grasp (lookin' at you creative types!) never fear! Schedules, like budgets, are easier made than one might expect, and setting goals actually relieves stress.

An important aspect of setting goals that relieve stress is to remain realistic. Humility comes into play when you are making realistic goals that you know you can achieve. Do not set your sights on the moon if you have not built your rocket ship! Setting and achieving realistic goals is of paramount importance when it comes to being the most successful person you can be. Success in every aspect of your life will work towards amassing your wealth; scheduling that success is important to ensuring it occurs!

Being self-sufficient is also important when it comes to maintaining motivation while pursuing your goals. Setting goals for yourself is the first step, attaining those goals will require many steps after it. Keep tabs on yourself to make sure you are accomplishing all that you need to be accomplishing. Nobody else is going to ensure you are working as hard as you can to achieve your goals.

Creativity is applicable to your schedule making in more ways than one. On the one hand, creatively deducing the best course of action could allow for you to come up with avenues of success that others had not considered. On the other, the ability to creatively solve problems as they arise is just as useful! The secret to being successful is not to never fail, it is to persevere through the failures until you reach the finish line. Sometimes this requires a little out of the box thinking, especially when you think you may be completely out of options. If you are the creative type it should come naturally to solve your problems creatively, but even if you are not, an introvert's tendency to spend time alone will oftentimes allot you plenty of time to consider your situation from every angle.

The bottom line is this: set goals. From daily goals to three, five, and ten-year plans, setting goals will give you the ability to set your sights on what needs to be done. More likely than not, when you set goals for yourself and begin reaching them, you will find new heights to scale. A perfect example of a successful introvert who continued to achieve his goals, and create new ones, is Bill Gates. Bill Gate's goal was to create both a computer and an operating system that was consumer friendly. These goals were quite lofty during the times that computers filled entire rooms. Bill Gates was known to spend days at a time working on his computers with his team, forever coming up with new and improved ways of transmitting data. His legacy today is a testament to the heights to which anyone, introverted or extroverted, can climb with enough determination to achieve their goals. To this day Bill Gates is investing in companies he sees worth in, giving to charities he believes in, and his company continues to produce software that allows billions of people to use their computers to their fullest potential. His impact on the world is substantial, and it all came from him having goals and sticking to them.

Make a five-year plan for yourself. You do not have to write it down, but keep it in mind. Think into your future; where do you want to be in five years? What sort of job would you like to have? How much money would you like to be making? How are you going to achieve these goals? When you start working backward from the future, you can turn your long term abstract goals into the daily schedule which you will need to follow to achieve those goals. That part you may want to write down.

Get yourself a planner and keep up with it. If your phone has a planner function, take advantage of it! Set alarms for yourself to remind yourself to exercise when you should be exercising every day. Make sure to put all your appointments into your phone or your planner so that you do not double book yourself or show up late. Keeping track of your life with diligence is the only way to ensure your success, so keep a schedule! After a certain time of planning your life, your physical reminders will fade from necessity as the habits will become parts of your daily life, but you still need to make sure that you are keeping some sort of calendar of your appointments. And make sure to schedule yourself down time! One of the worst parts of spending time doing "nothing" is the feeling that there is "something" that you should be doing. If you keep a schedule, one of the unsung joys is the ability to check off all the things you need to do, leaving you with nothing to do eventually. When you have done all you need for the day you get to enjoy the rewards of your hard work, namely the ability to relax and be comfortable in the home you work to maintain. By keeping your schedule, you end your days feeling accomplished instead of worried. You can also pencil in downtime throughout the day if you know you will be working long hours. When you have projects to get done, scheduling them in sections can help to keep from becoming overwhelmed. The benefits of scheduling are far reaching, so grab yourself some form of planner and get to it!

As for your long term goals, remember to keep them achievable. The trick to achieving long-term goals is to set yourself plenty of short term goals. When you continuously complete your short term goals, you not only make sure that you stay on the right path, but you give yourself little victories to celebrate. When you do accomplish goals it is important to take the time to celebrate your successes. It may seem inconsequential to celebrate simple accomplishments, or maybe even a little pretentious, but the truth of the matter is that celebrating your short term accomplishment lends credibility to the value of your long-term goals. If you gain real joy from completing your short term goals, the long term goal you have planned for yourself will be even more exciting, and the time you spend grinding towards it will be all the more worth it. If you find that you are not enjoying your accomplishments as much as you had expected to, it can give you an idea as to what you can expect once you reach the finish line. If you have to make a career change, better to do so as soon as you realize that the field you have chosen is not the right fit for you. Celebrating your little victories need not be anything grand, but the joy you feel should be allowed to flow. Indulging yourself in it will lend you strength on the dark days, so do not be afraid to get excited with yourself!

Another secret to amassing wealth is to genuinely enjoy what you do. The joy you feel when you are doing something you genuinely enjoy is a reward in and of itself, but when you do what you love for a living, there is a better chance you will pour your whole heart into it, and that shines through. Whether it is a creative endeavor or a sales invoice, someone who is enjoying doing what they are doing will be noticed. If you have to do things you don't enjoy, as is often the case, just make sure that you are set upon a path to eventual joy. Planning your goals and scheduling your life is how you make sure that you end up where you want to be, and everyone agrees that regardless of where they eventually end up, they want to be happy.

CHAPTER 7

FROM OBSERVATION TO IMPLEMENTATION

One of the most commonly described traits of an introvert comes from their interactions in social environments. It is often said of introverts that they seem to be scanning the room, taking it all in, watching and analyzing everyone. This is generally true of most introverts in social situations, as they are unlikely to be engaged in boisterous laughing or light-hearted conversation. The introvert's natural inclination is to stay in the background, observing everything around them and making calculations as to how best to proceed. This trait has led to many a great invention by introverts, most namely Facebook.

That's right, Mark Zuckerberg, CEO of Facebook is quite possibly the most famous introvert of this generation. Warren Buffett, Bill Gates, Mark Zuckerberg: the titans of their time. How did Mark Zuckerberg come up with his genius social media site? By observing a need and an opportunity, and taking it upon himself to seize the opportunity to fill that need. His social media site was developed with a tiny group of programmers to connect college students at the college he attended. His ingenuity in bringing the old campus tradition of a "face book" to the new computer age was soon adopted by colleges all across the country. Eventually, the invitation-only platform began allowing the invitation of college preparatory high schools, and soon after the whole world was connecting with Facebook, and Zuckerberg became a billionaire.

He saw a need, he filled the need. He saw the opportunity, he seized the opportunity. The ability to do this came from his introverted tendency to observe the world around him. In a world that seemingly has a new major app coming out every day, it may seem like every need is being filled, that every opportunity has been seized. Facebook seems like it came out of nowhere and conquered the social media realm, but in fact, it was once a competitor itself. Myspace and Xanga were very popular social media sites, with more customization features and less exclusivity than Facebook, yet Facebook managed to surpass them all in popularity over time. So if you have observed a way that you can fill a need, do not be discouraged by the fact that others are trying to do so as well. The market is unpredictable; if you pour yourself into your work you have just as much a shot as anyone else trying to make it.

As an introvert, you may notice that your natural tendency is to observe the world around you. The world around you is filled with opportunities yet to be discovered or things that can be done in a different way. When you observe these things, look at them as opportunities and consider how you can take advantage of them. It is okay to start small. Every opportunity is not a billion dollar idea. Is there a store in your neighborhood that doesn't carry a product that you would like to buy? Is it something that you can provide?

Rick Malley is not a famous man, but he is an introvert who used his powers of observation to start a successful small business. He was a bellhop at a local hotel on the Mississippi gulf coast who enjoyed to garden as a hobby. He was planting his spring garden and wanted to buy a specific type of pepper so he went to the local garden center and tried to purchase the plant only to learn that they did not carry that particular type of pepper plant. He tried several other local stores only to find that no one in the region carried the plant. After some research to make sure the plant would, in fact, grow in the climate where he lived he went to the local grocery store and purchased a few of his favorite peppers and after using them for cooking, he saved the seeds. There were several hundred seeds and after some research, he planted the seeds and the next thing he knew, he had several hundred small pepper plants. He took the plants to the local garden center and they bought them all. The idea worked and now he grows plants from seeds and sells them to local garden centers and other stores in his region.

This is just one example of something small that turned into a thriving business because of one person's ability to observe and implement. Following through is the key. If Rick had simply accepted the fact that his favorite pepper plant was not available in his area and bought something else instead, he would have never started a small business. Instead, he did something about it. He observed and implemented. As an introvert, your natural tendency to quietly observe is a blessing. Observation without implementation will get a person nowhere, but making an observation and taking action can lead a person anywhere.

As an introvert, your observation skills can be the perfect second set of eyes. Where most people can look at a situation or a set of problems over and over again without seeing a solution, the introvert's observation skills set them apart. Even the most observant, when faced with the same problem they have been considering for a while, begins to lose the ability to see new ways to solve their problems. Sometimes, consultants are hired to come in to fix problems because they are a new set of eyes on an old problem. Are you an ideal consultant? If you have an area of expertise, consulting may be the perfect career path for you as an introvert! A consultant does not have to spend a lot of time around large groups of people; they come in when they are needed, and they get out when they are done. A consultant's expertise is oftentimes unquestioned; if you are a good consultant your ideas will be appreciated enough by your clients to stand on their own merit, word will be passed throughout the industry by people who are impressed with what you do, and you will be able to be humble in your line of work and still be recognized. Being a consultant is one of the most self-sufficient career path choices one can make; their lifestyle is literally the monetization of their ability to fix problems. As was already mentioned, the come and go lifestyle of a consultant perfectly fits the introvert's desire to spend a considerable amount of their time in solitude. Also, if creative problem solving is your specialty, then being a consultant is again the perfect job for you! Being goal oriented and being able to schedule well is another talent that lends itself to a successful consulting business. A lot of times consultants will be hired because companies have fallen behind in their schedules and they need someone with powerful observational skills to help them realistically adjust their expectations.

Take a look at the world around you. What do you notice? Have you ever thought or told a friend that "they should" or "there should be" because you have observed a need? If you have, then you have observed without implementing. Put those observation skills to work for your success and you are on the way to cracking the code to success.

CHAPTER 8

MANAGING YOUR SUCCESS

O nce you crack the code to wealth, you are going to want to keep it. As you find yourself rising to higher levels of success financially and in other aspects of your life, it is important to understand how to stay there and continue to grow both financially and emotionally. Here are some important steps to ensure your success has a long shelf life:

- Do not isolate yourself. You may only have a few relationships, but they will be deep and meaningful. Work on building deep relationships with your family and friends and from time to time, add new relationships to your life. Personal relationships are as important as business relationships in maintaining a healthy life. By developing relationships in your business world, you may find that you are finding it easier to build relationships in your personal life. Of course, as an introvert, you are going to like your time alone, but make sure you spend good times with other people from time to time. Humans are social creatures by nature, and to have the healthiest life, one must not isolate one's self completely.

- Take care of your health. This is true of everyone but can be especially tricky to the introvert. Because the introvert does not like to spend too much time in public settings, especially around high energy people, a gym might be the last place you find an introvert. If you find that gyms are too intimidating for you, you will need to find other ways to keep your health up. Meditation and yoga can help you to stay mentally focused and healthy. Jogging is another way to stay fit. If you want to try to make it to the gym, try putting on headphones and see if that helps isolate you enough to make it through a workout routine. Dieting is another important factor to consider. Even if you do not want to get too into dieting, you need to watch what you eat. A balanced diet is better than nothing, even if you are not counting calories.

- Always seek to improve yourself. Take time for education and honing your craft. Warren Buffett's example of taking courses to further his education in areas that he was less skilled in is one you should take to heart. If you feel you have mastered one area of your craft, focus your attention on a new one. There is never a shortage of information these days, so never stop learning! Do not limit yourself to only learning about things you feel are related to your work either. If you get a wild idea to learn a completely new hobby, explore the thought! If you wake up one morning with a strong desire to paint, but no idea how to begin, research it! You may be as skilled as you need to be at work, but you can never know too many ways to have fun!

- Be kind to yourself. You are probably your worst critic. If you are an artist or musician, especially so. If you find yourself encountering failure on your road to success, try not think too long about them, only long enough to learn the lesson and move on. You are doing the best you can, and that is all anyone can ask. Nobody ever got anywhere because they beat themselves up enough. Learning from your mistakes is important, but beating yourself up is not the way to do so.

- Give yourself credit for your successes. As an introvert, others may overlook your because you are not seeking the spotlight, and extroverts may intentionally step in front of you into the light, but always give yourself credit and your work will speak for itself. This is how you manage to become boldly humble. By quietly congratulating yourself on your successes, your own appreciation of yourself makes you work harder, which in turn creates more and more successes. Even if it does not happen right away, you will eventually be given the credit you deserve by others if you continue to give it to yourself.

- Build a team. Unlike extroverts who need all the credit, introverts understand the value of a team. Build a strong team and keep them happy. Working together may not be your natural inclination, but it may be in the best interest to your success. Bill Gates does not run Microsoft alone. Find a good team to work with to accomplish your goals, and you will climb the ladder of success much faster.

- Communicate. More often than not, introverts are constantly talking to themselves. This inner dialogue is a part of why introverts feel so much more comfortable alone, their minds are always going. The downside to this inner dialogue is that sometimes it does not make its way out. Learn to communicate the important parts of your inner dialogue with your team, and your customers or clients. It is important they are kept up with what you have going on in your head, and since they cannot be in there with you, you have to talk it out with them.

- Be accessible. Set aside time to be accessible to your team and to your customers. Remember your planner?

If you are to be successful in life, you have to make sure that what you are doing is having its desired effect. The only way you will know it is doing so is if you make the time to hear back from the people involved in it. If your team has problems, or successes, to report, they need to be able to reach you at any time. If your customers have complaints or compliments, they also need to be able to be responded to in a timely manner. Having a business email is a good way to ensure that you are able to respond to everyone who needs your attention, so consider getting one.

- Carve out time for solitude. As you become more and more successful, solitude will become harder to find. The constant demands of a successful business will also create a greater demand for your time. Be careful not to sacrifice solitude. At the same time that accessibility is important, your battery recharging solitude is also very important. Do not sacrifice all of your alone time, as an introvert it will lead to you being less capable in the times you are in public, and that will not make anything better for anyone.

- Identify and stay connected with your support network. As an introvert, you are going to be generally more inclined to have a small network of people who you consider close. These people are going to mean a lot to you, though, and making sure that you are connected to them will become more and more important the more successful you become. It will also become more difficult as your time is needed for more and more business related matters. Just remember to stay connected to the people who were there for you when you were down, and the people who continue to be there for you when life gets rough. These people will also be the ones who celebrate your successes with you the most genuinely, so stay connected with them. It may seem mildly against your introverted tendency to be self-sufficient, but having a support group is important. Being self-sufficient means taking care of your own needs, but that is not always possible. You would not be able to perform your own open heart surgery, sometimes you are not able to solve every one of your problems.

- Learn to deal well with any setbacks that may occur. If things are not working out as planned, make sure you are not beating yourself up, but also make sure you are learning the best way to move forward. Learning to deal with setbacks is more than just emotional damage control. You need to be solving problems creatively if you are going to be successful. Sometimes taking a step back from it all may be necessary, sometimes a problem will require you to take a harder look at what you are doing. Being adaptable to your situations will be the best way to make sure you come up with the best solutions.

- Review your goals, set new ones if necessary. The process of setting goals for yourself should be a constant thing in your life. You do not make one grocery list in your life, you should not make only one list of goals. As you continue to grow, as time passes and you reach your goals, you should be always setting your sights on new horizons. Every hill you climb should give you a new mountain to consider. If you are to become a lone wolf tycoon, you can never be satisfied with where you are. This does not mean you cannot appreciate your hard work, it just means that you must stay hungry for success no matter how much of it you may have your fill of.

- Share your goals and the progress you have made in reaching them. There is a better chance that you will reach your goals if you have shared them with your support network. The idea is not to brag constantly about what you plan and what you do, the idea is simply to let those in your support group know about what you have going on in your life. Sharing your goals with others gives you not only motivation to stay focused, but it allows others the opportunity to give you valuable input in ways they see that you could improve. As we discussed in the chapter about being observant, an outside pair of eyes can often times see solutions that a pair who is super focused cannot. The same is true of your goals, someone close to you may have valuable insight to share on them, so keep them informed!

- Print out your goals. Printing your goals out, or writing them down, is a great way to turn these intangible ideas of the future into real world existences you can see and touch. Even though they are just words on paper, they are far more emphasized when they are physically in front of you. Make a few copies of your list of goals and hang them in places around your house that you will easily see and they will be quick reminders to keep you motivated in moving forward. Hanging them on the bathroom mirror is a great place, or on the fridge, or on your bedroom door. It may sound silly, but constantly reading your goals really can help to keep you focused.

Cracking the code to wealth will not happen overnight. It will take time, perseverance, and dedication. Make sure you are keeping yourself motivated. If you find it hard to keep yourself motivated, establish a support group to help keep your motivated. There will be times where you feel like giving up on your goals, this is another time the support group will come into play. Cracking the code to wealth is not easy, or everyone would do it. It will beat you down, you have to keep getting back up. Eventually, with enough hard work and determination, and a little good luck, you will find yourself becoming the lone wolf tycoon.

CONCLUSION

Thank for making it through to the end of *The Lone Wolf Tycoon: A Guide for Introverts to Crack the Code to Wealth.* Let's hope it was informative and able to provide you with all of the tools you need to achieve your goal of cracking the code to wealth. If you had any doubts about the ability of the introvert to become wildly successful, then hopefully this book has dispelled them. An introvert is only limited by his or her willingness to succeed. As you have learned throughout this book, an introvert is just as set up to succeed, if not more so, than any extrovert.

The next step is to begin setting your goals, making your budgets, and working towards becoming a lone wolf tycoon!

There's that old cliché: "Rome was not built in a day". The same is as true for your lone wolf business empire as it was for the Roman Empire so long ago. Inevitably, your empire will take time and dedication for you to see it to fruition. It will take patience, talent, and – admittedly – a fair amount of luck. However, if you make sure to make the best of your introvert character traits, you will have a firm foundation to build upon. There's no telling how prosperous and fortunate you could be with a simple combination of a strong foundation, some essential skills, a keen eye for niche opportunities, and a lot of patience, but all signs point to "very". I wish you luck on your journey to become the best businessperson you can be – not in *spite* of your introversion, but rather by taking full advantage of it.

If you like to hear about my other projects, please visit the address below.

http://clika.pe/l/13430/56723/

Finally, if you found this book useful in any way, a **review** on Amazon is *always* appreciated!

www.ingramcontent.com/pod-product-compliance
Lightning Source LLC
Chambersburg PA
CBHW050531210326
41520CB00012B/2528